Couscous with Rosemary and Wine Flavour ... 2
Mexican Style Couscous with Pineapple Chu... 3
Crabs with Couscous ... 4
Couscous Middle Eastern Style ... 5
Couscous Tagine with Aubergine ... 6
Mexican Style Couscous ... 7
Almonds with Raisins and Couscous ... 8
Asparagus-Mint-Couscous Mix ... 9
Chicken Broth Flavoured Couscous with Feta ... 10
Stir Fried Chicken with Couscous ... 11
Couscous with Beans and Vinegar ... 12
Couscous Bowl with Almonds ... 13
Couscous Muffins ... 14
Couscous with Squash and Beans ... 15
Couscous with Almonds and Tomatoes ... 16
Feta with Olives and Couscous ... 17
Quinoa-Couscous-Mix ... 18
Boiled Couscous with Asparagus ... 19
Greek Style Couscous with Feta ... 20
Chicken Breast with Couscous and Zucchini ... 21
Couscous with Curry and Raisins ... 22
Spicy Chicken with Carrots and Couscous ... 23
Couscous with Feta and Shrimps ... 24
Pepper-Lemon-Couscous-Mix ... 25
Cucumber-Lemon-Couscous Mix ... 26
Pork Chops with Mushrooms and Couscous ... 27

Couscous with Rosemary and Wine Flavour

Servings: 4

Ingredients:
250 ml water
80 ml white cooking wine
1 tbsp. butter
1/2 tsp dried rosemary, crushed
1/4 tsp salt
170 g couscous, regular or whole wheat

Directions:
1. Boil everything except the couscous for 2 mins then pour in the couscous, place a lid on the pot, and let the contents sit for 7 mins with no heat.
2. Fluff the couscous with a fork after all the liquid has been absorbed.
3. Enjoy.

Mexican Style Couscous with Pineapple Chunks

Servings: 2

Ingredients:

120 ml water
450 g (canned) pineapple chunks, drained (juice reserved)
170 g couscous
450 g (canned) black beans, rinsed and drained
100 ml additional warm water
2 tbsps. taco seasoning mix

Directions:

1. Boil 120 ml of water along with the pineapple juice then add in your couscous and place a lid on the pot after shutting the heat.
2. Let the couscous sit for 7 mins before stirring it.
3. Stir fry the beans and pineapple with taco seasoning plus 100 ml additional water for 8 mins.
4. Then top your couscous with the pineapple mix.
5. Enjoy.

Crabs with Couscous

Servings: 6

Ingredients:

2 tbsps. butter
3 tbsps. minced garlic
2 heads bok choy, chopped
450 g (canned) corn, undrained
600 g (canned) baby clams, undrained
250 ml clam juice
450 g (canned) diced tomatoes
500 ml water
1 cube vegetable bouillon
240 g couscous
150 g crabmeat
100 g heavy cream
60 ml lime juice
250 ml red wine
2 tsps. garlic salt
1 tsp ground black pepper

Directions:
1. Stir fry your bok choy and garlic in butter for 7 mins then add in: couscous, corn, bouillon, clams and juice, water, and tomatoes.
2. Set your heat to low and then add in: black pepper, crabmeat, garlic salt, cream, red wine, and lime juice.
3. Cook everything for 32 mins uncovered with low heat.
4. Enjoy hot.

Couscous Middle Eastern Style

Servings: 4

Ingredients:

2 tbsps. warm water
5 saffron threads, or more to taste
170 g couscous
250 ml vegetable broth
1 celery stalk, diced
40 g dried currants
2 tbsps. extra-virgin olive oil
1 tbsp. lemon juice
1 tsp harissa, or to taste
1/2 tsp ground cumin
Sea salt to taste

Directions:

1. Get a bowl, mix: saffron and warm water.
2. Boil your couscous in broth then shut the heat after placing a lid on the pot.
3. Let the contents stand for 7 mins before stirring the couscous.
4. Get a bowl, combine: sea salt, saffron mix, cumin, couscous, celery, harissa, currants, lemon juice, olive oil.
5. Place everything in the fridge for 35 mins.
6. Enjoy.

Couscous Tagine with Aubergine

Servings: 8

Ingredients:

2 tbsps. olive oil
8 skinless, boneless chicken thighs, cut into 1-inch/2 cm pieces
1 eggplant/aubergine, cut into 1 inch/2 cm cubes
2 large onions, thinly sliced
4 large carrots, thinly sliced
60 g dried cranberries
100 g chopped dried apricots
500 ml chicken broth
2 tbsps. tomato paste
2 tbsps. lemon juice
2 tbsps. all-purpose flour
2 tsps. garlic salt
1 1/2 tsps. ground cumin
1 1/2 tsps. ground ginger
1 tsp cinnamon
3/4 tsp ground black pepper
250 ml water
170 g couscous

Directions:
1. Get a bowl, mix until smooth: black pepper, broth, cinnamon, tomato paste, ginger, flour, cumin, and garlic salt.
2. Stir fry your chicken in olive oil until browned all over but still slightly uncooked. Now put the chicken into your crock pot along with the eggplant. Then add: apricots, onions, cranberries, and carrots.
3. Add the broth mix too.
4. For 5 hours cook with the high setting.
5. Now get a big pot and get your water boiling.
6. Once it is boiling pour in your couscous.
7. Get the mix boiling again, then place a lid on the pot and shut the heat. Let the couscous sit in the hot water for 7 mins. Then stir it.
8. When the chicken is finished serve over the couscous.
9. Enjoy.

Mexican Style Couscous

Servings: 15

Ingredients:

170 g couscous
1/2 tsp ground cumin
1 tsp salt, or to taste
350 ml boiling water
1 clove unpeeled garlic
450 g (canned) black beans, rinsed and drained
180 g (canned) whole kernel corn, drained
75 g finely chopped red onion
20 g chopped fresh cilantro
1 jalapeno pepper, minced
3 tbsps. olive oil
3 tbsps. fresh lime juice, or to taste

Directions:
1. Add boiling water into a mixture of salt and couscous in a large sized bowl, and cover it with plastic wrap before letting it stand for about ten minutes.
2. In this time, cook unpeeled garlic in hot oil over medium heat until it has turned golden brown.
3. Now mash this garlic and add it into the couscous along with black beans, onion, cilantro, corn, jalapeno pepper, olive oil, and lime juice.
4. Serve.

Almonds with Raisins and Couscous

Servings: 6

Ingredients:

500 ml water
170 g pearl (Israeli) couscous
1 tbsp. olive oil
75 g chopped yellow onion
1 shallot, chopped
6 cloves garlic, quartered
75 g golden raisins
30 g chopped oil-packed sun-dried tomatoes
60 g slivered almonds
1/2 tsp kosher salt/salt flakes
1/4 tsp ground black pepper
3 tbsps. lemon juice
1 tbsp. butter, softened

Directions:

1. Boil your couscous, uncovered for 14 mins in water.
2. Simultaneously stir fry your garlic, shallots, and onions for 17 mins in olive oil.
3. Now add: almonds, raisins, and tomatoes.
4. Cook for 7 more mins. Pour the couscous into the shallot mix and cook for 3 mins.
5. Add some: lemon juice, pepper, and salt.
6. Shut the heat and add in your butter, let it melt, before serving.
7. Enjoy.

Asparagus-Mint-Couscous Mix

Servings: 6

Ingredients:

340 g dry couscous
60 g chopped green onions
1 fresh jalapeno pepper, finely diced
2 tbsps. olive oil
1/2 tsp ground cumin
1 pinch cayenne pepper
1 pinch ground black pepper
500 ml vegetable stock
1 bunch asparagus, trimmed and cut into small pieces
150 g shelled fresh or thawed frozen peas
2 tbsps. chopped fresh mint
Salt and freshly ground black pepper to taste

Directions:

1. Get a bowl, mix: black pepper, couscous, cayenne, onions, cumin, olive oil, and jalapenos.
2. Get your peas and asparagus boiling in the veggie stock and then pour it into the bowl.
3. Stir the couscous into the liquid and place a covering on the bowl.
4. Let the mix sit for 12 mins then stir it.
5. Add some mint, pepper, and salt before serving.
6. Enjoy.

Chicken Broth Flavoured Couscous with Feta

Servings: 6

Ingredients:

500 ml chicken broth
300 g couscous
200 ml olive oil
50 ml fresh lemon juice
2 tbsps. white balsamic vinegar
20 g chopped fresh rosemary leaves
Salt and ground black pepper to taste
2 large cooked skinless, boneless chicken breast halves, cut into bite-size pieces
150 g chopped English cucumber
30 g chopped sun-dried tomatoes
70 g chopped pitted kalamata olives
75 g crumbled feta cheese
20 g chopped fresh Italian parsley
Salt and ground black pepper to taste

Directions:

1. Get your stock boiling then add in your couscous.
2. Place a lid on the pot and shut the heat.
3. Let the contents sit for 7 mins before stirring.
4. Blend: vinegar, olive oil, and lemon juice with some rosemary.
5. Now add some pepper and salt before continuing.
6. Get a bowl, mix: tomatoes, parsley, couscous, feta, cucumbers, and chicken.
7. Cover the couscous with the dressing and add a bit more if you like also add some more pepper and salt too.
8. Enjoy.

Stir Fried Chicken with Couscous

Servings: 4

Ingredients:

1 tbsp. olive oil
500 g skinless, boneless chicken breast halves, cubed
1 pinch monosodium glutamate (or some of your favourite herbs as a substitute)
6 tbsps. soy sauce
6 tbsps. brown sugar
1/2 tsp red pepper flakes, or more to taste
1 lime, juiced and zested
500 ml vegetable broth
170 g couscous
20 g chopped cilantro
4 wedges lime for garnish

Directions:

1. Get a bowl, combine: zest, soy sauce, lime juice, sugar, and pepper flakes.
2. Boil everything gently for 4 mins until it becomes sauce like.
3. Now stir fry your chicken until it is fully done in olive oil for 7 mins.
4. Add in your glutamate while it fries.
5. Then top everything with the lime sauce and continue stir frying for 4 more mins.
6. Let your couscous sit in the veggie broth that was boiling for 7 mins in a covered pot.
7. Place some couscous on a plate for serving and add a topping of lime chicken.
8. Garnish with freshly squeezed lime from the wedges.
9. Enjoy.

Couscous with Beans and Vinegar

Servings: 8

Ingredients:
170 g uncooked couscous
300 g chicken broth
3 tbsps. extra virgin olive oil
2 tbsps. fresh lime juice
1 tsp red wine vinegar
1/2 tsp ground cumin
8 green onions, chopped
1 red bell pepper, seeded and chopped
20 g chopped fresh cilantro
180 g frozen corn kernels, thawed
900 g (canned) black beans, drained
Salt and pepper to taste

Directions:
1. Get your broth boiling for 2 mins then add in your couscous.
2. Place a lid on the pot and shut the heat.
3. Let the couscous sit in the hot water for 7 mins, before stirring it.
4. Get a bowl, mix: beans, olive oil, couscous, corn, lime juice, cilantro, vinegar, red pepper, onions, and cumin.
5. Add your preferred amount of pepper and salt. Then place a plastic covering around the bowl, let the mix sit in the fridge for 20 to 30 mins before serving.
6. Enjoy.

Couscous Bowl with Almonds

Servings: 6

Ingredients:

130 g creamy salad dressing
60 g plain yogurt
1 tsp ground cumin
Salt and pepper to taste
1 tbsp. butter
75 g couscous
250 ml water
1 red onion, chopped
1 red bell pepper, chopped
20 g. chopped parsley
50 g raisins
35 g toasted and sliced almonds
100 g (canned) chickpeas, drained

Directions:
1. Get a bowl, combine: pepper, salad dressing, salt, cumin, and yogurt.
2. Cover the bowl with some plastic wrap and chill in the fridge for 1 hour.
3. Simultaneously toast your couscous in butter for 2 mins then add your water.
4. Get everything boiling, then place a lid on the pot, set the heat to low and let the contents gently boil for 7 mins.
5. Get your dressing mix and add in: chickpeas, couscous, almonds, red onions, raisins, parsley, and bell peppers.
6. Place the covering back on the bowl and put it back in the fridge for 20 mins.
7. Enjoy.

Couscous Muffins

Servings: 10

Ingredients:

300 g coarsely chopped zucchini
230 g coarsely chopped onions
1 red bell pepper, coarsely chopped
500 g extra lean ground turkey
75 g uncooked couscous
1 egg
2 tbsps. Worcestershire sauce
1 tbsp. Dijon mustard
110 g barbecue sauce, or as needed

Directions:

1. Coat your muffin pan with non-stick spray or grease with cooking oil; and then preheat your oven to 400°F/200°C.
2. Blend with a few pulses: bell peppers, zucchini, and onions. Then add them to a bowl, with: mustard, turkey, Worcestershire, eggs, and couscous.
3. Evenly divide the mix between the sections in your muffin pan then add bbq sauce to each (1 tsp).
4. Cook everything in the oven for 27 mins.
5. Check the temperature of each, it should be 160°F/70°C.
6. Let the dish sit for 10 mins before serving.
7. Enjoy.

Couscous with Squash and Beans

Servings: 4

Ingredients:

2 tbsps. brown sugar
1 tbsp. butter, melted
2 large acorn squash, halved and seeded
2 tbsps. olive oil
2 cloves garlic, chopped
2 stalks celery, chopped
2 carrots, chopped
200 g garbanzo beans, drained
75 g raisins
1 1/2 tbsps. ground cumin
Salt and pepper to taste
450 ml chicken broth
170 g uncooked couscous

Directions:

1. Preheat your oven to 350°F/180°C.
2. Cook your squash for 32 mins in the oven. Then top the squash with a mix of butter and sugar that has been melted and stirred together.
3. Stir fry, for 7 mins, in olive oil: carrots, celery, and garlic.
4. Now add the raisins and beans.
5. Fry the contents until everything is soft then add in pepper, salt, and cumin.
6. Add the broth to the carrot mix and then add the couscous.
7. Place a lid on the pot and place the pot to the side away from all heat.
8. Let the contents sit for 7 mins.
9. Fill your squashes with the couscous mix.
10. Enjoy.

Couscous with Almonds and Tomatoes

Servings: 3

Ingredients:

250 ml water
1 tsp dried savory
1 tsp dried parsley
1 pinch crushed red pepper flakes
1 tbsp. chicken bouillon granules
85 g pearl (Israeli) couscous
1 lemon, zest grated
55 g toasted slivered almonds
20 g chopped celery
50 g chopped onion
1/2 tomato, seeded and chopped
1 tbsp. olive oil
Salt and black pepper to taste

Directions:

1. Boil the following for 2 mins: bouillon, savory, pepper flakes, and parsley.
2. Now add the couscous and let it gently boil with a lower level of heat for 12 mins.
3. Place a lid on the pot and shut the heat.
4. Once the couscous has lost its heat remove any liquid that is left.
5. Get a bowl, combine: olive oil, zest, tomato, almonds, couscous mix, onions, and celery.
6. Add your preferred amount of pepper and salt and the place the contents in the fridge for at least 30 mins covered with plastic wrap.
7. Enjoy.

Feta with Olives and Couscous

Servings: 3

Ingredients:
60 ml chicken broth
120 ml water
1 tsp minced garlic
80 g pearl (Israeli) couscous/ptitim
20 g chopped sun-dried tomatoes
30 g sliced Kalamata olives
2 tbsps. crumbled feta cheese
200 g (canned) garbanzo beans, rinsed and drained
1 tsp dried oregano
1/2 tsp ground black pepper
1 tbsp. white wine vinegar
1 1/2 tsps. lemon juice

Directions:
1. Boil your garlic in the broth for 3 mins. Then add in your couscous.
2. Place a lid on the pot and shut the heat.
3. Let the couscous sit in the hot water for 7 mins and then stir it.
4. Get a bowl, combine: black pepper, beans, vinegar, tomatoes, oregano, lemon juice, cheese, olives, and couscous.
5. Stir the mix and serve at room temp.
6. Enjoy.

Quinoa-Couscous-Mix

Servings: 8

Ingredients:
1.7 litre water, divided
170 g red quinoa
170 g pearl (Israeli) couscous/ptitim
200 g farro
1 cucumber, seeded and chopped
1/2 red onion, chopped
1 orange bell pepper, seeded and chopped
1 yellow squash, seeded and chopped
120 ml extra-virgin olive oil
1 lemon, juiced
1/2 tsp kosher salt/salt flakes
180 g crumbled feta cheese

Directions:
1. For 2 mins boil your quinoa in 500 ml of water. Then place a lid on the pot, set the heat to low, and the let quinoa cook for 17 mins.
2. Simultaneously cook the couscous in 350 ml boiling water for 12 mins in a covered pot.
3. At the same time boil your farro for 26 mins in remaining water, in a covered pot as well.
4. Once everything is done get a bowl, combine: squash, quinoa, bell peppers, couscous, onions, cucumber and farro.
5. Top with a dressing of: salt, lemon juice, and olive oil.
6. Place a plastic covering over the bowl and cool it in the fridge for 1 hour.
7. Before serving top the salad with some feta.
8. Enjoy.

Boiled Couscous with Asparagus

Servings: 4

Ingredients:

340 g couscous
1 bunch fresh asparagus, trimmed and cut into 2-inch/5 cm pieces
240 g grape tomatoes, halved
180 g feta cheese, crumbled
3 tbsps. balsamic vinegar
2 tbsps. extra-virgin olive oil
Black pepper, to taste

Directions:
1. Boil your couscous in water, then place a lid on the pot, shut the heat, and let the couscous sit for 7 mins.
2. Once it has cooled stir it with a fork.
3. Simultaneously steam your asparagus over 2 inches/5 cm of boiling water with a steamer insert and a pot. Steam the spears for 7 mins. Now remove all the liquid.
4. Get a bowl, toss: couscous, olive oil, asparagus, balsamic, cheese, pepper, and tomatoes.
5. Enjoy chilled or warm.

Greek Style Couscous with Feta

Servings: 20

Ingredients:

180 g garlic and herb couscous mix
1 pint cherry tomatoes, cut in half
150 g jar pitted kalamata olives, halved
175 g mixed bell peppers (green, red, yellow, orange), diced
1 cucumber, sliced and then halved
20 g parsley, finely chopped
240 g crumbled feta cheese
130 g Greek vinaigrette salad dressing

Directions:

1. Get your couscous boiling in water for 2 minutes. Then place a lid on the pot, shut and heat, and it sit for 7 mins before stirring after it has cooled.
2. Place the couscous in a bowl, and combine in: cheese, tomatoes, parsley, olives, cucumber, and bell peppers.
3. Add in your Greek dressing and toss everything to coat evenly.
4. Feel free to add more dressing if you like.
5. Enjoy.

Chicken Breast with Couscous and Zucchini

Servings: 6

Ingredients:

170 g whole wheat couscous
1 tbsp. vegetable oil
1 medium onion, chopped
2 bay leaves
5 whole cloves, crushed
1/2 tsp cinnamon
1 tsp ground dried turmeric
1/4 tsp ground cayenne pepper
6 skinless, boneless chicken breast halves - chopped
480 g (canned) garbanzo beans
480 g (canned) crushed tomatoes
1.5 litre chicken broth
2 carrots, cut into 1/2 inch/1 cm pieces
1 zucchini, cut into 1/2-inch/1 cm pieces
Salt to taste

Directions:
1. Get your couscous boiling in water for 2 minutes. Then place a lid on the pot, shut and heat, and it sit for 7 mins before stirring once it has cooled.
2. Stir fry your onions in oil until soft then add in: cayenne, bay leaves, turmeric, cloves, and cinnamon.
3. Cook everything for 1 more min then pour in your chicken and cook it until browned all over.
4. Once everything has been browned add in: broth, tomatoes, and beans.
5. Get everything boiling.
6. Lower the heat to low and gently boil for 27 mins.
7. Now add your zucchini and carrots and also some salt.
8. Continue for 12 more mins.
9. Serve the veggies and chicken over the couscous.
10. Enjoy.

Couscous with Curry and Raisins

Servings: 6

Ingredients:

250 g couscous
750 ml chicken stock
1 tbsp. curry powder
2 tsps. salt
1 tsp ground black pepper
2 tbsps. extra-virgin olive oil
75 g raisins
1 bunch cilantro, chopped
55 g slivered almonds, toasted

Directions:

1. Boil the following then pour it over your couscous in a salad bowl: raisins, stock, olive oil, curry powder, pepper, and salt.
2. Place some plastic wrap around the bowl, and let the couscous stand for 12 mins before stirring it.
3. Serve the couscous with some almonds and cilantro.
4. Enjoy.

Spicy Chicken with Carrots and Couscous

Servings: 4

Ingredients:

800 ml low-sodium chicken broth
170 g quick-cooking couscous
2 tbsps. olive oil
4 skinless, boneless chicken breast halves - cut into cubes
1 pinch ground black pepper
50 g finely chopped jalapeno chili peppers
1 carrot, thinly sliced
1 zucchini, diced
3 green onions, thinly sliced
1 1/2 tsps. grated fresh ginger root
1 1/2 tsps. curry powder
1/2 tsp ground coriander seed
1 tsp corn-starch

Directions:

1. Boil 2/3 of your broth and then add the couscous and olive oil. Place a lid on the pot and let the contents sit for 12 mins.
2. Get a bowl, mix: corn-starch, remaining broth, and curry.
3. Coat your chicken with pepper then stir fry it in 1 tbsp. of olive oil until fully done.
4. Remove the chicken from the pan.
5. Add in more olive oil and stir fry carrots and jalapenos for 4 mins then add: broth, zucchini, ginger, and onions.
6. Cook everything for 7 more mins.
7. Add your corn-starch mix and cook for 3 more mins.
8. Serve the spicy chicken and carrots over the couscous.
9. Enjoy.

Couscous with Feta and Shrimps

Servings: 8

Ingredients:

340 g couscous
500 ml water
200 ml olive oil
60 ml apple cider vinegar
1 tsp Dijon mustard
1 tsp ground cumin
1 clove garlic, crushed
Salt and pepper to taste
1 red bell pepper, chopped
1 yellow bell pepper, chopped
750 g cooked shrimp, peeled and deveined
2 medium tomatoes, chopped
20 g chopped fresh parsley
150 g crumbled feta cheese

Directions:

1. Boil your water then pour in your couscous, place a lid on the pot, and then let it sit for 7 mins and finally stir it once cooled.
2. Get a bowl, combine: pepper, olive oil, salt, garlic, vinegar, and mustard.
3. Get a bigger bowl, mix: cheese, shrimp, parsley, couscous, tomatoes, and bell peppers.
4. Now combine in the vinegar mix and toss everything to coat.
5. Place the mix in the fridge for 1 hour then serve.
6. Enjoy.

Pepper-Lemon-Couscous-Mix

Servings: 4

Ingredients:
2 tbsps. butter
2 tbsps. olive oil
4x 120 g salmon steaks
1 tsp minced garlic
1 tbsp. lemon pepper
1 tsp salt
60 ml water
200 g chopped fresh tomatoes
20 g chopped fresh cilantro
500 ml additional boiling water
170 g uncooked couscous

Directions:
1. Coat your salmon with salt, lemon pepper, and garlic.
2. Now begin cooking it in olive oil and butter.
3. Then add 60 ml water, cilantro, and tomatoes. Place a lid on the pan and cook for 16 mins.
4. Simultaneously boil 500 ml of water and add in the couscous. Place a lid on the pot and cook for 7 mins.
5. Top your salmon and couscous with any sauce in the pan when serving.
6. Enjoy.

Cucumber-Lemon-Couscous Mix

Servings: 8

Ingredients:

300 g uncooked couscous
2 tbsps. olive oil
120 ml lemon juice
3/4 tsp salt
1/4 tsp ground black pepper
1 cucumber, seeded and chopped
60 g finely chopped green onions
20 g fresh parsley, chopped
15 g fresh basil, chopped
6 leaves lettuce
6 slices lemon
500 ml water

Directions:

1. Boil water; then pour in the couscous.
2. Let it boil for 2 mins before placing a lid on the pan and setting it to the side for 7 mins.
3. Stir the contents after it has cooled off a bit.
4. Get a bowl, mix: pepper, oil, salt, cucumber, couscous, onions, basil, parsley, and lemon juice.
5. Serve the couscous over leaves of fresh lettuce and add some lemon as a topping on each plate.
6. Enjoy.

Pork Chops with Mushrooms and Couscous

Servings: 4

Ingredients:

1 tbsp. vegetable oil
4 boneless pork chops, 3/4-inch/2 cm thick
1 clove garlic, minced
320 g (canned) Cream of Mushroom Soup
120 ml milk
700 g hot cooked couscous

Directions:
1. Stir fry your pork for 12 mins in oil and then remove it from the pan.
2. Add in your milk and soup. Heat it until everything is boiling.
3. Once it is boiling put the pork back in the pan and lower your heat to a simmer.
4. Cook everything covered for 12 mins or until the pork is completely done.
5. Enjoy over the couscous.

Image sources/Printing information
Pictures cover: depositphotos.com;
@ CogentMarketing; @asimojet; @studioM; @ Nadki
Print edition black and white paperback:
Amazon Media EU S.à.r.l.
5 Rue Plaetis
L-2338 Luxembourg
Other printouts:
epubli, a service of neopubli GmbH, Berlin
Publisher:
BookRix GmbH & Co. KG
Sonnenstraße 23
80331 München
Deutschland

Printed in Great Britain
by Amazon